Revelation's Three MOST WANTED

Mark Finley
and Steven Mosley

Pacific Press® Publishing Association
Nampa, Idaho
Oshawa, Ontario, Canada
www.pacificpress.com

Cover design by Fred Knopper
Photo Credit: Digital Vision, Dynamic Impressions,
MetaPhotos, and ThinkStock

Additional copies of this book are available by calling toll free
1-800-765-6955 or visiting
http://www.adventistbookcenter.com

ISBN: 0-8163-1997-9

03 04 05 06 07 • 5 4 3 2 1

Contents

Conspiracies vs. God's Plan

Deep in the woods, some people are training with assault rifles, preparing for the day when black helicopters swoop down from the sky and take away all human liberties. Some are stockpiling cans of food in their basements, preparing for the day when all public utilities shut down and services are paralyzed.

Why? Why are some people driven to stockpile food or take to the woods with a rifle? For many, it's because they believe conspiracy theories.

Conspiracy theories clearly have a powerful appeal today. They spread even in times of relative calm and prosperity. They claim to give the *real* explanation, the *real* picture of what's going on. They claim to give us a peek at the *real* movers and shakers behind the scenes.

But what makes the difference between believing that black helicopters are about to swoop down on us or believing the latest theories about the antichrist and end-time events? What makes the difference between those who see conspiracies everywhere and those who see God's plan?

In this chapter, I'd like to look at what conspiracy thinking does to our heads and our hearts. I'd like to look at how we can live in a world of evil and suffering and disaster—and still hang on to the perspective of faith. How do we believe in a divine plan in such a world? Does faith mean seeing fewer conspiracies, or more?

The first thing we need to understand about conspiracy theories is that they fill a need in people's lives. Some individuals are drawn to theories of conspiracy; they just latch on to them.

Dr. Gregory Schneider, professor of behavioral science at Pacific Union College in Angwin, California, has looked at how conspiracy theories have shaped individuals and groups all through history. "When I hear people talk about conspiracy theorists," Dr. Schneider says, "I often think about a kind of 'us-against-them' mentality. The 'us' is always righteous, or more righteous, than the often purely evil, but powerful, mysterious people that you've got to watch out for."

Conspiracy thinking binds people into a close-knit group. It's "us against them." Those who are caught up in these theories feel that they have to stick together because there are so many bad guys out there. And there's comfort in that. It creates a strong identity.

"Some people are going to be attracted to conspiracy theories because a lot of conspiracy theories tell you how something will occur," says Herb Helm, former therapist and now a psychology professor at Andrews University in Michigan. "Therefore you have more control in that element. In other words, if you know the future, you don't have to have as much anxiety about it as you do if you're a little ambivalent about what's going to happen to you in the future."

Conspiracy theories offer a complete explanation of all the details. Everything that is happening is the result of certain forces at work. And *you* know what they're planning to do! Believing you have that inside information satisfies a human need for control. That's why some individuals find conspiracy theories so compelling. It isn't just facts begging for an explanation; it is hearts crying out for security.

Now, here's where people start getting into trouble. People want to be sure. People want to be secure. And they often use conspiracy theories to be absolutely sure—about everything. "One of the characteristics of the closed mind," declares Dr. Schneider, "is that it has an explanation for everything. Any piece of data, any news item, any fact or story that threatens the fundamental belief is neutralized." So conspiracy thinking tends to be very self-contained. It alone has the real explanation. All other explanations, no matter how plausible, are the result of that vast conspiracy, that vast plot to pull the wool over our eyes.

Another problem with conspiracy thinking is that it tends to demonize opponents. People on the other side aren't just mistaken; they aren't just imperfect. No! They are part of that terrible, dark plot; they are part of the forces of evil!

Church historian George Knight has documented various ways this kind of thinking can be harmful even in the Christian church. "It does sometimes tend to get people a little off-center," Knight says. "Sometimes they look for the devil rather than the solution or the real problem. Too often conspiracy theorists identify a person or a movement as being the problem of the world; they see things in terms of black and white."

Conspiracy thinking looks for enemies; it looks for someone to blame. And that can result in tragedy. Throughout history, terrible things have been done to groups and individuals who were identified as the "real" threat, the "real" problem.

Around the time of the Great Depression and before the Second World War, a number of fundamentalist thinkers believed in a conspiracy of international Jewish bankers and other supposedly wealthy Jewish people who were directing the Roosevelt administration. So when Roosevelt attempted to combat Nazism through alliances of convenience with the Soviet Union, Christian fundamentalists at that time saw this as Roosevelt doing the bidding of his Jewish advisors. A really ugly anti-Semitism arose that tended to discredit Christian love and charity. In some cases, Christians came close to being on the side of the Nazis with their extreme anti-Semitism. Conspiracy thinking can do great harm. It can make demons out of our enemies. It can push us to extremes.

This brings us to a dilemma. To some people, the Christian worldview itself seems to be a part of this kind of conspiracy thinking. After all, don't Christians believe the devil is lurking out there in the dark, working behind the scenes, manipulating leaders and institutions, plotting to harm us? Don't Christians believe in a great conspiracy of dark forces arrayed against us? And what about the antichrist? What about the beast and the dragon portrayed in Revelation? They certainly seem to be part of a cosmic conspiracy in the end times.

So what's the difference between the perspective of the Bible and typical conspiracy thinking? Is there any difference? Are they one? Dr. George Knight points us to an answer: "In the very foundation of Scripture itself there is a metaphysical scheme—the existence of forces of good and forces of evil—which I believe is true. The problem comes when we tend to focus on the forces of evil and don't balance that out with Christian responsibility and the positive side of the plan that God has for His people." Conspiracy thinking puts the forces of evil on center stage so that they fill up the horizon. The enemy becomes the focus of attention. However, in the Bible, it is God's plan that takes center stage. He's the One who is bringing history to a climax.

Let's take a look at something the apostle Paul tells us in his letter to the Ephesians. He's talking about the central character in the Bible, the One who fills up the horizon:

He [God the Father] worked in Christ . . . and seated Him at His right hand in the heavenly places, far above all principality and power and might and dominion, and every name that is named, not only in this age but also in that which is to come (Ephesians 1:20, 21).

You see, Christ is enthroned high above all principalities, high above all powers, high above all dominions. Are there forces of evil at work in our world?

Certainly. Are there principalities of darkness at work? Certainly. But the New Testament emphasis is on the fact that Christ has won the battle over all these powers. He was victorious in His life on earth. He was victorious in His death. He was victorious in His resurrection.

At the Seventh-day Adventist Theological Seminary in Berrien Springs, Michigan, Bible scholars have delved deeply into the book of Revelation. They've made the study of end-time events a specialty. And they've discovered that certain key elements distinguish the writers of the New Testament from the creators of conspiracy theories today. Dr. John McVay, New Testament professor and dean of the Seminary, states:

Most conspiracy theories feature a cover-up in which the conspirators are out to hide the real truth. They want to keep the public from knowing what is really going on. But in the New Testament and its story of the second coming of Jesus, we have displayed the exact opposite: God is seeking again and again to communicate to humanity the idea that He is returning, that He is coming back.

Someone has called natural disasters, the footsteps of an approaching God. If we understand God's movement through history, He's trying to communicate in a variety of ways this idea that He's coming back, He is going to bring a grand end to human history.

Second, most conspiracy theories involve disaster because once the story unfolds, once the information is out, it's worse than you could have ever imagined. It's far worse; it's an utter disaster.

In the Bible story of the return of Christ, again, it is just the reverse. In the Bible, the situation turns out to be far better than you could have ever dreamed. The return of Christ, the end of human history as God has planned it, is a wonderful, tremendous event to which all of us—those whose worldviews are informed by Scripture—look as the grand hope of humankind.

Are we focused on disasters or are we focused on God's great plan? That makes the difference between being dominated by conspiracies and having great hope.

The New Testament calls the climax of history, the second coming of Christ, the "blessed hope." Here's how the apostle Paul put it: "We wait for the blessed hope— the glorious appearing of our great God and Savior, Jesus Christ" (Titus 2:13, NIV). This Jesus, the great Savior who died for us, is coming to this world again. That is our "blessed hope."

Yes, we face many uncertainties from day to day. But one thing is certain: We are headed toward the day of Christ's "glorious appearing." Yes, political events can throw our world into turmoil, but we can still know that history is heading toward one climax—the second coming of Christ. This is the blessed hope—a living hope—that can be an anchor for our souls.

Dr. Keith Mattingly, chairman of the Department of Religion at Andrews University, says:

> I look at the Old Testament prophets, and they talk about a holocaust that will come, an apoca- lypse. But they see the coming holocaust as some-

thing that will stop the horrors around us so that we can enter into a time of peace that comes afterward—a peace in which the trees clap their leaves, a peace in which we can see the old men sitting at the city gate, see children playing and people eating of the fruit of their own planting, see a heaven that is full of rest and peace and joy. That's something to look forward to!

Let's look at the way Psalm 96 describes God's coming to judge the earth at the end of time:

> Let the heavens rejoice, let the earth be glad; let the sea resound, and all that is in it; let the fields be jubilant, and everything in them. Then all the trees of the forest will sing for joy; they will sing before the LORD, for he comes, he comes to judge the earth. He will judge the world in righteousness and the peoples in his truth (Psalm 96:11-13, NIV).

The psalmist can barely contain his excitement. The prospect of his Lord's return makes him exult. It fills him with praise. He's jubilant. All nature seems to be celebrating before his eyes. For the Hebrews, God the Judge was God the Vindicator. He would vindicate their cause, rule in their favor. His coming didn't represent the end, but a new beginning. The Hebrews looked forward to the glorious kingdom that God Himself would set up.

And that perspective grows even brighter in the New Testament because that's where Christ, the Messiah, takes center stage. That's where He is lifted up as the great hope of human beings. And Jesus continued to be a blessed hope for believers even in the worst of times. Early Christian believers could have easily been consumed by gloomy conspiracies. "In New Testament times people had to deal with the power of Rome, which was a very brutal, repressive dictatorship governed by the man at the top who was the emperor. There were all kinds of bad things going on in those days," says Dr. Roy Gane, professor of biblical interpretation at the Seventh-day Adventist Theological Seminary. "But the early Christians rose above all that and focused upon Christ. For them, to die was a wonderful thing because they knew that the next thing they would know they would be with Christ and would be redeemed."

New Testament believers were not intimidated by the power of Rome. They didn't spend their time theorizing about what dark principalities and powers might be doing behind the scenes. They celebrated the risen Christ—the name that was enthroned above every other name.

Dr. Gregory Schneider sees a stark contrast between this perspective and the kind of conspiracy thinking that is always on the lookout for enemies, the kind of thinking that generates fear. "It seems to me," he says, "that what characterizes a strong, healthy Christian life is confidence, hope, and peace. If you're constantly fearful, that kind of thinking really doesn't further the Christian spiritual life."

Scripture assures us that the climax of history will be the glorious appearing of Jesus—not some overwhelming disaster. The New Testament shines with that blessed hope. And it calls us to a certain kind of life as a result of that hope. It calls us to a life of service. That's the exact opposite of the life of those who hunker down in some stockpiled bunker, waiting for the conspiracy to crash down on them. It's the opposite of a life of fear and self-protection.

George Knight says:

> There's a built-in tension in the New Testament itself between the "signs-of-the-times" approach—let's sit on the edge of the chair waiting for Jesus to come—and the "occupying-till-I-come" approach. We find it in Matthew 24 and 25. We tend to focus in Matthew 24 on the signs of the times that are given there, but if we keep reading, that chapter talks about waiting. And what are we supposed to do while we wait? Use our talents. How do we use our talents? We feed the hungry. We visit those who are in jail. We help the bereaved.

The apostle Peter talks about the second coming of Christ as an event that separates things of ultimate value from things that aren't. He describes the elements melting away and the heavens disappearing with a roar. Then he says, "Since everything will be destroyed in this way, what kind of people ought you to be? You ought to live holy and godly lives as you look forward to the day of God and speed its coming" (2 Peter 3:11, 12, NIV). What is the only thing that remains after the apocalypse? Godly lives. Everything is removed except our relationship with God. Wealth, position, power, connections—they won't mean anything. The only thing that will matter is the quality of our life with God, the quality of what we do for others.

Dr. Schneider has seen evidence, down through history, of individuals and groups, who have combined a great hope in Christ's coming kingdom with great lives of service in the world, people who have had their heads in the clouds, but their feet firmly on the ground. He says:

One example, that gives me inspiration is the story of Fernando and Anna Stahl. The Stahls were Seventh-day Adventist missionaries to Indians in the highlands of the Andes in Peru. Now, Adventists are certainly people who are expecting the soon coming of Christ, nevertheless the Stahls settled down and gave themselves for decades to the lives and problems and concerns of the Indians.

They clearly saw their efforts as part of building up the kingdom of God and themselves as agents of the soon-coming kingdom. They saw their work as part of the process of building a kingdom that Christ will eventually come and complete. On that score, I think Anna and Fernando Stahl were not only living spiritually healthy lives, they were also living lives of effective service and helping to build what Adventists call the "blessed hope."

Is your life filled with a blessed hope today, or are you weighed down with worries, anxious about conspiracies, focused on enemies? Are you experiencing the abundant life that Jesus Christ promised to all those who follow Him, to all those who eagerly await His appearing?

I invite you to come to Him right now. He'll change your perspective. He'll get your eyes off the difficulties and problems of the world. He'll change the focus of your attention from conspiracies and evil powers and wicked forces and demons and unions of church and state. He will focus your eyes upon Himself.

He is the all-powerful Christ, the everlasting Christ. You need not fear. You can place your life in His hands. You can give Him your future. His plans are better than yours. His plans are grander than anything you can dream up. Allow Jesus Christ to take center stage in your life. Give Him His rightful place above every principality and power. Give Him your fears, give Him your heartaches, give Him your longings, give Him your future right now as we pray.

* * * * *

Dear Father, I praise You for holding out such a bright hope for us in the New Testament. Thank You for giving us Your perspective on the future. We want to make the Lord Jesus Christ the center of our lives, right now. We want to make His plans, our plans. So we place our faith in Him. Take our lives. Mold them according to Your will. We want to live in the blessed hope. In Jesus' name, Amen.

New Terror, Old War

From the rubble of a shocking terrorist attack on America, a new resolve rose in the hearts of men and women all across the land—a resolve to deal with terrorism once and for all. The world is being introduced to a new kind of war that will require a new kind of commitment. But, as we shall see, success in dealing with evil once and for all depends on understanding where we stand in a very old war, a war that's been waged for thousands of years.

September 11, the day three passenger planes crashed into the World Trade Center and the Pentagon, changed the world forever. That's the only way we can express the profound shock we feel. Something happened on September 11 that propelled us into a new kind of fear, a new kind of sorrow, a new kind of war.

World leaders have expressed a resolve to strike at the root of worldwide terrorism. Are we going to be successful? How long will it take? How much will it cost—in human lives? Will we ever feel truly safe again? These are questions that are running through our minds, and yes, sometimes keeping us awake at night.

In this chapter, I'd like to try to answer the questions: Can we deal with evil once and for all? And if so, upon what does our success depend? I'd like to try to answer those questions by looking at a very old conflict. Because the new war on terrorism is very much related to an old war. The fiery explosions we see on the evening news are very much related to a conflict behind the scenes, a conflict that determines the nature of all other conflicts.

Let me start by showing you a day that changed life on our planet forever. This was a day that began in Paradise and ended in terror. The book of Genesis tells us that Adam and Eve, our first human parents, enjoyed freedom and prosperity in the Garden of Eden. It was a place of beauty. It was a place of plenty. But there was one creature hanging around who just couldn't stand this couple's happiness. One day he struck out at them with a seductive lie. God had warned them to stay away from the tree of the knowledge of good and evil. But the creature told them its fruit would make them as wise as God Himself!

When Adam and Eve tasted that forbidden fruit, they experienced something they'd never felt before—terror and fear. "Then the LORD God called to Adam and said to him, 'Where are you?' So he [Adam] said, 'I heard Your voice in the garden, and I was afraid because I was naked; and I hid myself'" (Genesis 3:9, 10).

Adam and Eve had always enjoyed a face-to-face friendship with God in the Garden. His voice had been a welcome sound. But now something had changed. Now they were afraid. Now they felt guilty. Now they wanted to hide. Sin entered the world on that terrible day long ago, and life on this planet would never be the same. Our relationship with God would never be the same.

Now there would be conflict. Now there would be animosity. Now there would be a struggle to survive. Now there would be terror.

Do you know what lies at the root of terror? An inability to trust, a break in trust. If we don't trust God to take care of us, we'll try to get our needs met by any means necessary. Terrorism is really an attempt to find security by any means necessary. It's the extreme opposite of trusting God to take care of your needs. Now we're getting to the heart of a conflict that's been going on for a long, long time. Adam and Eve bought into the lies of someone who wanted to destroy their happiness. They began to believe that God was holding something out on them. They stopped trusting Him.

Who was this creature who seduced Adam and Eve in the Garden of Eden? Well, he was a more dangerous being than they could ever have imagined. He was a fallen angel who had actually managed to start a war in heaven. His name was Lucifer, "Son of the Morning." He had occupied a privileged place near God's throne. But he allowed jealousy to seep into his soul. He became disconnected. All this glorifying of the Almighty started getting under his skin.

Lucifer wanted all of God's perks. He wanted the applause. He wanted the glory. Lucifer became obsessed with his position. Jealousy turned to poison in his heart. And he began to believe that he could be completely fulfilled only if he got God out of the way. So what happened?

The book of Revelation tells us that the war on earth began actually in heaven: "And war broke out in heaven: Michael and his angels fought with the dragon; and the dragon and his angels fought, but they did not prevail. . . . So the great dragon was cast out, that serpent of old, called the Devil and Satan, who deceives the whole world; he was cast to the earth, and his angels were cast out with him" (Revelation 12:7-9).

Lucifer's jealousy turned into such hatred that he was willing to go to war against God, against Christ and His angels. He persuaded other heavenly beings that God was holding something back; that He wasn't fair; that He couldn't really be trusted; that they would be better off on their own.

Lucifer pictured God as the enemy. All his discontent and frustration focused on one thing—getting out from under God's control. Overthrowing God's rule was worth any sacrifice—that's what he talked himself into believing. It was worth starting a conflict he couldn't hope to win. It was worth spoiling heaven itself.

Lucifer lost that first great cosmic battle. He and his allies were deported from the heavenly courts. And he set up camp here on earth. Here is where he hoped to start another insurrection. And that's why he appeared to Adam and Eve, trying his best to persuade them that God couldn't be trusted, trying to persuade them to believe they just had to get out from under God's thumb.

Friends, terror here on earth started with a war in heaven. Suicide bombers and murderers of the innocent go straight back to that first anarchist, Lucifer. His basic problem is at the root of terrorism today.

Take some of these terrorists. They have an excellent education. They have strong financial backing, and they have all the right connections in all the right places. They could do extreme good in the world. But instead they spend their time and energy and resources creating vast networks of terror. They've focused their energies on murdering and maiming civilians by the thousands.

Why? Because all their misdirected fervor and religious fanaticism is focused on one thing, one enemy— Western civilization. The United States and other Western nations are so powerful, their influence is so widespread, that terrorists have persuaded people that getting out from under the West's thumb is worth any sacrifice. It is even worth starting a war they couldn't hope to win. No measure is too extreme.

Now, there's certainly a lot of poverty, corruption, and injustice in the world. There are wrongs to right. There are things to fight for. And I'm sure the United States and the rest of the Western world have made some mistakes in their foreign policies.

But the terrorists have pictured the Western way of life as the source of all evil. They imagine that getting rid of those influences will bring peace and fulfillment to the rest of the world. That goal, they feel, is worth any price. It's worth training children in acts of terrorism. It's worth sending devoted followers on suicide missions of murder. For them, it's worth blowing up embassies and office buildings. It's worth thousands of innocent lives snuffed out in one day.

I believe jealousy and resentment turn to poison in fanatics who become terrorists. Let me say it plainly: I believe terrorism is the direct descendant of Lucifer, the first being who let his pride turn into hatred.

Satan has brought the war in heaven to earth. Satan, that roaring lion, has been waging a campaign of terror on this planet for thousands of years. That's his style. He uses coercion. He uses intimidation. He uses fear.

That's the challenge that faces us. We're seeing acts of terror that are just the latest flare-ups in a long and deadly war. How can we respond effectively? Is there a realistic hope of dealing with terror once and for all?

The prophet Isaiah gives us a startling glimpse of what was going on in the courts of heaven long ago:

"How you are fallen from heaven, O Lucifer, son of the morning! How you are cut down to the ground, you who weakened the nations! For you have said in your heart: 'I will ascend into heaven, I will exalt my throne above the stars of God; I will also sit on the mount of the congregation on the farthest sides of the north; I will ascend above the heights of the clouds, I will be like the Most High' " (Isaiah 14:12-14).

"Why should God be the center of everything?" Lucifer questioned. He started resenting, instead of enjoying, God's glory. He didn't understand the nature of God's tremendous love.

That love puts the voices of hatred to shame. That love pushes the ranting of fanatics into the shadows. God's love is what stands now. God's love has been standing through eternity. God's love will remain standing in the end.

As Paul warned us, "Being puffed up with pride," we "fall into the same condemnation as the devil" (1 Timothy 3:6). The jealous try desperately to exalt themselves. God went to great lengths to humble Himself as a man, as a servant. The proud look for enemies to blame. God looks for believers to justify.

Satan has desperately tried to crush out God's light, wherever it's lifted up on the earth. He tried over and over to destroy the nation of Israel. They were the first to show the world who the God of heaven and earth really is. They passed on God's principles of justice and mercy and truth.

And what happened? Egypt's Pharaoh enslaved them. He did his best to crush their spirit and their faith.

The empire of Assyria invaded Israel.

The empire of Babylon burned Jerusalem.

And Satan did more than attack God's people from the outside. He also attacked them from the inside. He used the jealousy and resentment of Hebrew kings and princes and priests to terrorize courageous prophets such as Isaiah and Jeremiah. Those who lifted up God's voice were hunted down and thrown into dungeons and sometimes killed.

Centuries later, God began spreading the light of the gospel through the early Christian church. Satan, that raging dragon, was quick to attack. He tried to trample this blossoming faith through fiery persecution. Some of the Roman Caesars did their best to terrorize the first believers into submission.

And through the years, Satan has attacked the church from the inside as well. The powerful church of the Middle Ages sometimes turned persecutor. Earnest nonconformists were tortured and burned. Priests actually turned to terror as a means of conversion.

That's the way it's been. The war in heaven has spilled out on earth. Lucifer's spirit of jealousy and mistrust infects human beings. People focus their frustration on an enemy. They must get rid of some group in order to be happy, in order to be at peace. It's worth any cost, any sacrifice.

The new war on terrorism requires an investment of time. It requires a major commitment. And that points to the heart of God's response to terrorism, His response to Lucifer's challenge. This is the key component to success in dealing with evil in our world today. This is God's answer. This is His move against jealousy and resentment and hatred. This is how He reacts to being regarded as the enemy.

To put it simply, God didn't fight the war from a distance. He came close. God got His hands dirty. That's the commitment He made in the person of Jesus Christ. And that's the good news that we can cling to in the face of terror.

Here is how the apostle Paul expresses it: "Grace to you and peace from God the Father and our Lord Jesus Christ, who gave Himself for our sins, that He might deliver us from this present evil age" (Galatians 1:3, 4).

God wants to deliver us "from this present evil age." He wants to deliver us from its terrors. How does He do that? He gives up Himself for our sins. He did that in Christ on the cross. He became a casualty. He absorbed all that we fear in His own body. He absorbed all the world's misdirected hatred in His own flesh.

In the book of Romans, Paul sheds further light on what the Cross means. He says:

> God presented him [Christ] as a sacrifice of atonement, through faith in his blood. He did this to demonstrate his justice, because in his forbearance he had left the sins committed beforehand unpunished—he did it to demonstrate his justice at the present time, so as to be just and the one who justifies those who have faith in Jesus (Romans 3:25, 26, NIV).

There is so much truth in these words. The atonement has meaning on so many levels. But let's consider what it means in the long war. One thing that was established on the cross was God's justice, God's righteousness. He had been accused; He had been slandered. Propaganda had been passed around that human beings must get out from under His thumb to be fulfilled.

Well, God in Christ answers all those charges on the cross.

Does God simply order us around from a distance? By no means! He came to shed His blood for us! Is God looking for a way to condemn, to keep us in our place? By no means! He died to pay the penalty for our sin. Does God have to control everybody to be happy? By no means! He gave up His life in order to give us our freedom.

God made a spectacle of His love and mercy and justice on the cross. It was His ultimate act of counterterrorism. He exposed the ugliness of sin for what it is. On the cross, as a victim of violence, Almighty God demonstrated that violence is not the answer. He gives His love to us, and it's that love—His sacrificial love—that gives Him the right to be our sovereign Lord.

So, the real question for you and me today, in the midst of a war on terrorism, is this: Where do we stand when it comes to God's love? As a nation we have to defend ourselves from murderous fanatics. We have to protect the innocent from terror. Sometimes tough love is required. We have to do our best to seek out the murderers and bring them to justice—with as little loss of life, of course, as possible.

But there's also the question of our response as individuals. And that's extremely important. Because if we really want to deal with terrorism and evil once and for all, we're going to have to recognize some painful truths about ourselves. We're going to have to recognize that the spirit of that original terrorist in the Garden of Eden can strike very close to home. The enemy can find aid and comfort right in our own hearts.

Let me give you a specific example. Listen to Paul's admonition in Ephesians 4:26, 27. " 'Be angry, and do not sin': do not let the sun go down on your wrath, nor give place to the devil."

What is Paul saying here? He's saying, "Be angry." Sometimes anger is an appropriate response. It's OK to be angry when fanatics kill thousands of innocent human beings. Outrage is a normal response of the human heart.

But Paul also says, "Be angry, *and* do not sin." Don't let anger turn into sin. Don't hang on to it until it hardens into hatred, into an obsession with revenge. That's important, because if that happens we "give place to the devil."

We can give the enemy a place in our hearts, just as Adam and Eve gave him a place in the Garden of Eden—with disastrous results. How? He gains a place when we buy into hatred, when we center our lives around enemies, instead of God.

That's why Paul gives this urgent appeal, a few verses later: "Let all bitterness, wrath, anger, clamor, and evil speaking be put away from you, with all malice" (verse 31).

Put away hatred and resentment and jealousy. That's actually the stuff of terrorism. Terrorists are simply people who express these qualities on a large scale, a global scale. They are simply people who have the means to express their hatred dramatically.

Friends, the real war on terrorism has to begin in our own hearts. We have to understand that individual human sin, that fractured relationship with God, is behind the suffering and tragedy in this world. We can't afford to give in to the jealousy and resentment that drove Lucifer from heaven.

The cosmic war between good and evil is going on right now in our inmost thoughts, our own impulses. And we need to decide for sure where we stand when it comes to God's love.

The book of Hebrews tells us exactly what to do in

order to stand in the right place. It pictures Jesus Christ as a great High Priest, the One who justifies those who respond in faith, the One who can deal with the sin inside of us. And then we find this invitation: "Let us draw near with a true heart in full assurance of faith, having our hearts sprinkled from an evil conscience" (Hebrews 10:22).

"Let us draw near." We need to get close to the One who can cleanse our hearts from animosity and jealousy. We need to get close with a true heart, an honest heart. God didn't battle against evil from a distance. He didn't just send down a surgical strike force from heaven. God Himself came close. God Himself got involved. God Himself got His hands dirty.

We need to respond in kind. Have you been keeping God at a distance? Have you been just nodding your assent to the right beliefs? It's time to do more than that. There's a war going on. And it's a war that must be won in our own hearts.

I challenge you, today, to draw near. Get involved with God; start a real, open-hearted, straight-talking, eye-to-eye relationship with God. Get your hands dirty. Deal with the stuff in your inmost heart. And when you deal with the stuff in your inmost heart, it becomes a struggle, friend; it becomes a fight.

But it's a battle Jesus promises to win on your behalf. In this war, the enemy has already been decisively defeated at the Cross. So please, draw near. Draw near to the One who has earned the right to be your Rescuer. Draw near to the One who has earned the right to be your Champion, your Savior, your Lord, your mighty Deliverer.

All around us we see the battle between good and evil, right and wrong, the forces of light and the forces of darkness. We feel that battle in our own minds. We sense that battle in our own hearts. We see it in our own families.

But there is a way to be victorious in that battle. Christ cast Lucifer out of heaven millenniums ago. He won! And Christ can win the battle in your life. But the only battle He can win is the one you let Him fight for you.

Would you like to do that today? Would you like to say, "Jesus, I'm weak but You're strong. Jesus, You can win the battle for me. Jesus, I turn my life over to You right now for time and eternity"? Would you like to do that as we pray?

* * * * *

Dear Father, thank You for coming close to us. Thank You for invading the camp of the enemy, in the person of Jesus Christ. We want to remove all the obstacles now, everything that stands between You and our hearts. We give You our trust. We give You our future. We give You each day. Thank You for the sacrifice You made to deal with the problem of evil once and for all. Thank You for your gracious forgiveness. We commit ourselves to You right now in the name of Jesus Christ our Lord. Amen.

The Roar of Pride

They flash into view through the fire and smoke of events just before the world's end. They are history's last and biggest villains—three shadowy figures who gain tremendous power in the end times. The book of Revelation identifies them by code words: the beast, the false prophet, the dragon.

If God had "wanted" posters, these are the characters who would be up on the wall. It's important for us to understand "Revelation's Three Most Wanted," because they represent the end time's most dangerous sins. They embody those things that are essential for each of us to overcome.

The book of Revelation comes to us from an island called Patmos where the apostle John recorded the remarkable visions he was given toward the end of his life. It's a book of dramatic contrasts. It's a book of conflict. It looks at history—past, present, and future—as a moral battlefield.

In Revelation we find a number of contrasts or parallels. There is:

• A pure woman, Christ's church, versus a gaudy prostitute, representing apostate religion.

- A sea of glass versus a lake of fire.
- A call to "worship the Almighty" versus a call to "worship the beast."
- The Lamb who was slain versus the dragon who slays.

But in all these parallels, there is one that escapes most people's attention. Revelation actually presents us with an unholy trinity. It's a threesome that wars against the Holy Trinity of Father, Son, and Holy Spirit.

We first see the members of this unholy trinity together in Revelation 16:13. Here's what the apostle John writes: "And I saw three unclean spirits like frogs coming out of the mouth of the dragon, out of the mouth of the beast, and out of the mouth of the false prophet" (Revelation 16:13).

Each of these three figures has an unclean spirit. It's something as repulsive as a frog coming out of someone's mouth. But each of these figures manages to attract a huge, worldwide following. People fall down and worship them. That's what we discover as we continue to read what John wrote about them. So, although they have a specific unclean spirit, they are very seductive, very charismatic figures. They don't seem repulsive to most people. Remember that Satan himself can dazzle the world, appearing as an angel of light. That is what is ahead of us as history comes to a climax—three star villains, each having a specific way he will try to seduce and deceive.

In order to make it through this coming crisis safely, we need to understand exactly what these three figures are trying to do. I believe God has given us clues regarding this unholy trinity and the end time's most dangerous sins. He can enable us to avoid them. He can keep us in a safe place through all the deception and seduction of the end time.

In this book, we're going to take on Revelation's "Three Most Wanted." We're going to discover just what "unclean spirit" each one will manifest. The keys are in the Bible. Our loving God has shown us how we can avoid the fate of the unholy trinity. Each one of them is eventually thrown into the lake of fire. But our Father has different plans for us. He wants us celebrating in heaven with all those He rescues from this doomed planet.

So let's get started. Let's look at the first star villain in the book of Revelation.

The beast occupies center stage in the drama of the apocalypse. He's the one who is most dazzling. He causes thousands and thousands of people to fall down and worship him. Just what is the "unclean spirit" this figure projects onto the world? What's the sin behind his seduction?

Let's look at how the beast makes his entrance; it's recorded in Revelation 13:1. John writes, "Then I stood on the sand of the sea. And I saw a beast rising up out of the sea, having seven heads and ten horns, and on his horns ten crowns, and on his heads a blasphemous name."

This powerful figure is, to put it simply, decked out. He's decked out with symbols of power. One crown isn't good enough; he has to have ten of them! And he's taken his high position to an extreme; he actually has blasphemous names on his heads! Revelation 17:3 pictures him as a beast "which was full of names of blasphemy."

What is blasphemy? Jewish leaders accused Jesus of blasphemy when He claimed to be able to forgive sin. "Only God can forgive sins," they said. They failed to grasp the fact that Jesus was indeed God in the flesh. Blasphemy is trying to take God's place. It's claiming to be able to do what only God Himself can do. So the beast's "names of blasphemy" are claims to be able to do what only God can do. The beast, then, is a religious figure who tries to exalt himself to the level of the Almighty.

What is the beast's "unclean spirit"? It's pride, pure and simple. Pride pushed to the limit. That's what drives the beast. That's what he uses to try to get to us.

We have a striking example of this in Daniel—the Bible's other book of apocalyptic prophecy. Daniel includes the remarkable story of Nebuchadnezzar's mental collapse. The king of Babylon actually became like a beast. He started crawling around in the fields, chewing on grass. His hair grew long and matted. His fingernails grew into claws.

Why? What drove Nebuchadnezzar over the edge? The story is in Daniel 4. One day this monarch was walking around his royal palace, admiring the awesome hanging gardens and temples in the city. And this is what he said: " 'Is not this great Babylon, that I have built for a royal dwelling by my mighty power and for the honor of my majesty?' While the word was still in the king's mouth, a voice fell from heaven: '. . . your dwelling shall be with the beasts of the field' " (Daniel 4:30-32).

Pride drove this king mad. It turned him into a beast. It happened in ancient Babylon. And it will happen again in the Babylon of the end times. The roar of the beast in Revelation is the roar of pride. That's what makes him so dangerous.

Do you know why? Because he grabs at something that lurks inside the hearts of all of us. He touches our egos. The beast of Revelation isn't just some wild figure of fantasy. He's not inhuman. He's someone who's a lot closer than we think.

The writers of the New Testament make a point to warn about the sin of pride. Here's what the apostle Peter says: "Be clothed with humility, for 'God resists the proud, but gives grace to the humble' " (1 Peter 5:5). And the apostle Paul emphasizes that love—the most important quality in the Christian life—is not proud. And he tells Timothy that one of the perils of the last days is that men will be proud.

Why is pride such a problem? Why is it one of the most dangerous sins in the end times?

Because pride pushes God away. Pride builds a defensive wall. Pride won't let God get to our needs. And it's this human tendency that the beast makes the most of. This is his way of taking us captive in the end times. The beast is the final, terrible manifestation of the sin of pride. And at the same time, the beast exploits human pride.

How does that work? Let's look at Revelation 13. Here is how John describes those who become followers of this charismatic figure: "And all the world marveled and followed the beast. . . . And they worshiped the beast, saying, 'Who is like the beast? Who is able to make war with him?' And he was given a mouth speaking great things and blasphemies" (Revelation 13:3-5).

People marvel at the beast. Why? Because he smashes all his opponents. Because he compels thousands to bow the knee. It appears no one can resist him. No one can "make war with him."

In Second Thessalonians, Paul tells us that in the end time, "the man of sin" "opposes and exalts himself above all that is called God" (2 Thessalonians 2:4). Here we find an echo of Lucifer, that angel in heaven who tried to exalt himself above the throne of God. There is something inside the human heart that responds to this kind of power. In fact, it's the proud human heart that responds the most. It would seem on the surface, that the opposite should be true. Proud people should instinctively turn away from those individuals or powers that are the proudest, the most overbearing, right? You'd think that the proud would want only the humble around them, only the meek. That they would always want to be top dog.

But in fact the proud are irresistibly drawn to the beast. They see in this powerful, ruthless figure someone they ache to be like. He expresses their secret longings. He lives out their fantasies. The proud are often frustrated. They never quite get the recognition they think they should. Well, here's an opportunity to share in the great power of the beast. Here's an opportunity to rise to the top and dominate. That's why they worship the beast. They don't worship because they are humble. They don't worship because they love. They worship because they identify with this figure who overpowers all opposition.

Revelation shows us just what kind of coercion this involves.

> He causes all, both small and great, rich and poor, free and slave, to receive a mark on their right hand or on their foreheads, and that no one may buy or sell except one who has the mark or the name of the beast, or the number of his name. (Revelation 13:16, 17).

This is how pride roars. This is how pride expresses itself. "You can't buy or sell unless you're on my side." "You will be shut out unless you play by my rules." "You will have no rights unless you swear allegiance to my group."

You can hear the faint echo of that roar even today. You can hear it even in places that celebrate freedom the most passionately. The roar of pride finds an echo in the darker corners of the human heart. That fearsome beast expresses the desire that so many have held in secret—the desire to dominate, the desire to control.

But let's remember one thing—the beast is a religious power, part of an unholy trinity. He represents the new Babylon, a religion that attempts to counterfeit the faith of Jesus Christ. The beast who dazzles the world wants to replace the Lamb of God who takes away the sin of the world.

So let's think about how religion itself can be seduced by pride. That's really the heart of the matter. Now we're zeroing in on the thing we must avoid at all costs in the end time. How is religion seduced by the roar of pride?

Again, Revelation gives us important clues. Here is the beast again, showing his true colors: "Then he opened his mouth in blasphemy against God, to blaspheme His name, His tabernacle, and those who dwell in heaven. And it was granted to him to make war with the saints and to overcome them" (Revelation 13:6, 7).

Religion is supposed to take us to God, right? It's supposed to help us worship God. So how can it sink to the level of blasphemy?

By trying to take God's place.

Sometimes a church claims exclusive rights to God's name. Sometimes a church leader claims to speak for Him. "Only our messages bring His voice to earth," they claim. "Only our rituals bestow forgiveness. Only ours is the true tabernacle. Only ours is the true franchise of saints and angels, those who dwell in heaven." That's what a church can begin to believe.

Church leaders may think they're acting for the good of believers. They may persuade themselves they're just trying to protect the flock. But, my friends, in their lofty claims, in their elaborate ceremonies, you can hear a faint rumbling sound. It's the roar of pride. It's the sound of a beast awakening.

You may find that hard to believe about a church you dearly love, about a tradition that means a great deal to you. But history shows us it's already happened. The beast was once awakened even in Christendom.

One March day in 1546, George Wishart was brought before a solemn meeting of bishops at St. Andrews Abbey in Scotland. George had been preaching to people out in the fields even though the church had forbidden him to do so.

The interrogator, John Lauder, accused George of heresy.

George replied that he'd been speaking about the Ten Commandments, the Lord's Prayer, and the letter of Paul to the Romans.

Lauder pointed out that Wishart had done so "without any authority of the church." Then he began shouting, "Thou false heretic, traitor, and thief, deceiver of the people, thou despisest the holy church."

George replied, "We ought to obey God rather than men."

Lauder continued presenting evidence of heresy. George had taught that the Gospels urge us to confess our sins to God, not to a priest. George had questioned infant baptism, asking, "Shouldn't a person understand what he's committing himself to?"

George had declared that the Communion bread was just a symbol; it didn't actually become the literal body of Christ. George had questioned the practice of praying to saints, since the Bible clearly states we should worship God alone.

In other words, George was disagreeing with all these bishops in their impressive robes, seated in their imposing cathedral.

So Lauder shouted even louder, "Thou wilt not obey our general . . . councils."

George replied simply, "Without the express witness of the Scripture, I dare affirm nothing."

But that wasn't enough for the churchmen at St. Andrews. They couldn't allow this man to challenge their authority. They couldn't allow him to go on demonstrating that their cherished traditions had no basis in Scripture. And so they condemned him to be burned as a heretic.

In the fire that consumed this honest Scottish soul, we can hear the roar of the beast, the roar of pride. Tragically, there have been many other fires and many other victims. The beast has awakened many times in history. It has awakened in Christian churches. Leaders of the church have indeed made war with the saints.

And the book of Revelation tells us clearly that the beast will awaken again. It will awaken in the last days, roaring more loudly than ever, compelling human beings to give it allegiance.

Religion can fall to pride. It can try to take the place of God. And that's why we must make sure that the roar of pride finds no echo in our hearts. We must be sure that we're humbled before a holy God and not just identifying with a powerful, charismatic figure.

Revelation gives us a wonderful picture of those who are *not* seduced by pride, this most dangerous of end-time sins. "And I saw something like a sea of glass mingled with fire, and those who have the victory over the beast, over his image and over his mark and over the number of his name, standing on the sea of glass, having harps of God" (Revelation 15:2).

What are these people doing who overcome the beast? They're singing praises. They declare, "Great and marvelous are Your works, Lord God Almighty!" (verse 3).

They're opening up in true worship. They're not building walls in pride.

They're losing themselves in admiration. They're not clawing to the top in envy.

They're focused on the love of the Lamb. They're not boasting in the wealth of their tradition.

That's what's going to make all the difference.

I pray that you will keep true worship alive in your heart. Please, don't be seduced by the roar of pride. Don't let it draw you into a religion of "us against them." That won't bring you security. That won't bring you peace.

Keep your eyes fixed on the One who took on our human frailty, the One who humbled Himself to the point of death at Calvary. Keep your faith focused on the One who says, "You win the crown, by taking up the cross." Submit to His gracious guidance, and He will lift you up.

* * * * *

Lord, we know that the terrible roar of the beast is coming. And we know that it won't sound terrible at all to a lot of people. So come into our hearts now—into every dark corner—and deal with our pride, deal with our resistance, deal with our defenses. We come to You without any credentials, without any recommendations. We come empty-handed with our needs and our longings. Receive us. Forgive us in the name of Jesus Christ. Keep us close. Keep us teachable. Keep us trusting humbly in Your grace. Amen.

The Whisper of Complacency

In the great clash of events at the end of the world, three particularly dangerous characters stand out. They appear vividly in the book of Revelation—as a warning of what we must avoid at all costs.

In this chapter, we're going to focus on the second figure in this unholy trinity—the false prophet. He's perhaps the most seductive of all. He doesn't have the roar of the beast that we looked at in the last chapter. Instead, he comes with the whisper of someone promising miracles. We're going to discover just what magic he uses to compel millions to give him their allegiance.

Everybody loves magicians. We always want to see what they're going to pull out of the hat next. Canes turning into doves with a wave of the hand. Caged tigers turning into beautiful women in a puff of smoke. People apparently sliced in half—and put together again. Objects disappearing right in front of our eyes.

Magic is sure to draw a crowd. And magicians keep

finding more and more spectacular ways to capture—or misdirect—our attention. These days magicians are making the Statue of Liberty or an aircraft carrier disappear! Now they're doing stunts in midair. Now they're dazzling a whole city by spending days in a block of ice.

Magic tugs at our sense of wonder—"How did he do that?" It touches our desire for the miraculous—"That's unbelievable!" It suggests we can beat impossible odds. Maybe we can even cheat death.

The great magician and escape artist, Harry Houdini, died in 1926. One of the pallbearers at his funeral was a Broadway producer, Charles Dillingham. As he was helping carry the coffin out of the church, Dillingham leaned across to another pallbearer and whispered, "I'll bet you a hundred bucks he ain't in here!"

A way of escape. A way to transcend space and time. That's what magicians seem to offer. And that's why they keep us mesmerized.

Well, the book of Revelation tells us one thing about magic: False miracles are going to deceive many, many people. In the end times, a charismatic figure is going to rise up who will dazzle the whole world with his magical touch. Thousands will say they've seen great miracles with their own eyes. This is the picture the apostle John gives us of the false prophet as recorded in Revelation 19: "Then the beast was captured, and with him the false prophet who worked signs in his presence, by which he deceived those who received the mark of the beast and those who worshiped his image" (Revelation 19:20).

The false prophet is an ally of the beast, the powerful religious figure who tries to take the place of God on earth. The false prophet deceives people. He works to draw people into a false religious system. And he does this by performing signs. He's a wonder-worker. That's what John pictures.

Jesus Himself predicted the same thing. In Matthew 24 Jesus talks about what will happen before His second coming: "For false christs and false prophets will rise and show great signs and wonders to deceive, if possible, even the elect" (Matthew 24:24). "Great signs and wonders." That's how false prophets deceive. And the false prophet of Revelation is the greatest magician of them all, the greatest wonder-worker. He will perform signs that people will swear no one could do—except someone who truly represents God.

But let's look a bit closer at this false prophet. Let's find out exactly why he's a member of Revelation's "Three Most Wanted." Why do so many follow him? After all, God has His wonder-workers as well. Sometimes the Almighty performs miracles through sincere believers. In fact, Creation itself is one big wonder. And the way the Holy Spirit transforms human hearts is a dazzling sign.

So, why do so many fall for the signs and wonders of the false prophet? What does he have that's so seductive?

To get an answer, let's look at what the Bible has to say about false prophets in general. As it turns out they're almost always pictured in one particular way. They prey on one particular human weakness. We can see a great example in the story of Ahab and Micaiah.

In the third year of his reign, godly King Jehoshaphat traveled up north to visit King Ahab of Israel. Ahab suggested that the two of them join forces and recapture the town of Ramoth Gilead. It had been taken by the king of Aram.

Jehoshaphat was willing. But first he asked that they seek counsel of the Lord.

Well, Ahab happened to have four hundred palace prophets to call on. They were ushered in, and Ahab asked them, "Shall I go to war against Ramoth Gilead or shall I not?"

The men responded: "Go, for the Lord will give it into your hand."

Jehoshaphat was a bit suspicious of all these eager-eyed prophets. So he asked, "Isn't there a prophet of the Lord here whom we can inquire of?"

Ahab frowned. Yes, there was one man who claimed the right credentials. But he had a very negative attitude. Micaiah, son of Imlah, had never said one good thing about Ahab. Jehoshaphat thought the man should be summoned anyway, and Ahab reluctantly consented.

While Micaiah was on his way, the four hundred hired voices tried to be even more convincing and worked themselves into a frenzy. "Attack Ramoth Gilead and be victorious!" they shouted. One man put on a pair of iron horns, danced around, and declared, "With these you will gore the Arameans until they are destroyed."

Finally Micaiah arrived. There he stood in a palace before the two monarchs in their royal robes and four hundred chanting prophets. Ahab asked Micaiah what message he had from the Lord. Now, this prophet had a difficult choice to make. There was tremendous pressure to go with the flow, to conform to the consensus.

But Micaiah just couldn't bring himself to lie. Truth was something that God personally revealed. It wasn't something to be decided by acclamation. And so this brave, lone prophet gave a straight answer: "I saw all Israel scattered on the mountains, as sheep that have no shepherd" (1 Kings 22:17).

It wasn't a very encouraging message. Ahab turned to Jehoshaphat and complained, "Didn't I tell you? He never prophesies anything good about me."

But Micaiah kept going. He stood before the hundreds of disapproving prophets and told Ahab that they had become lying spirits leading him toward disaster. In the end, Ahab didn't listen. He sent God's prophet off to prison, stubbornly marched off to battle, and met the disaster Micaiah had predicted.

This story shows us exactly what a false prophet does. He tells us only what we want to hear. He indulges our desires. He flatters our egos. He strokes our prejudice. False prophets give our whims a green light. This happened during the ministry of the prophet Jeremiah, too. He was surrounded by false prophets who told Israel what the people wanted to hear: "You will be delivered from Babylon." No one wanted to heed Jeremiah's warning about a coming disaster. Here is one of God's warning messages that Jeremiah delivered: "The prophets prophesy falsely, and the priests rule by their own power; and My people love to have it so. But what will you do in the end?" (Jeremiah 5:31).

The people "love to have it so." They're hearing only what they want to hear. They're comforted. They're re-assured. But in the end they will be totally unprepared. Here is Jeremiah again: "Your prophets have seen for you false and deceptive visions; they have not uncov-ered your iniquity" (Lamentations 2:14).

False prophets don't help us deal with our problems. They don't break through our denial. They don't un-cover iniquity. They just tell us that everything is OK. They dispense cheap peace. They make easy promises when they should be giving urgent warnings.

Now we've come to the heart of the matter. Now we can see why the false prophet of Revelation seduces so many. He's going to be telling people exactly what they want to hear. He's going to be telling them everything will be OK if they will just stick with the crowd follow-ing the beast.

That's why the false prophet's signs and wonders work so well. It's a magic people *want* to believe in. They want to believe because they like what they're hearing. The false prophet's magic is a kind of misdi-rection. It says, "Look over here; pay attention to the special effects, the amazing phenomena. Don't look too closely at the message. Don't uncover the lies within the promises. Don't pick out the dangerous beliefs be-hind the nice words."

Do you remember Jim Jones who led the People's Temple? He dazzled his congregation with the mi-raculous. His members were caught up in what seemed to be signs of the Spirit. And they stayed mesmerized—all the way to that tragic mass suicide in Guyana.

In the end times, too many people will settle for magic, instead of truth. That's what Revelation is warning us about. This second figure of Revelation's "Three Most Wanted" is showing us one of the end time's most dangerous sins. Do you know what it is?

Complacency. Smugness. Self-satisfaction.

That's the human weakness the false prophet exploits. Human nature doesn't want to hear the hard truth. It doesn't want to be disturbed. If given a choice between truth and good news, it will always pick the good news.

That mysterious, charismatic figure of the false prophet isn't as removed as you might think. He isn't just an apocalyptic symbol in the distance. He's not inhuman. He's someone who's a lot closer than we imagine.

What he says will sound very plausible. The false prophet will make his magic seem so reasonable. He'll say something like this:

I'm here to tell you, friends, that all you have to do to know the truth is just to open your eyes. Look to the miracles. That's proof enough for me. Listen to what I'm saying now. Everybody goes around saying, "The Bible says this; the Bible says that." Sure, all that exposition is good, but why not let the divine miracles judge for today, for right now?

What have you seen and heard? The man who says he couldn't feel his tumor anymore. The woman whose leg grew out. The paralyzed gentleman who began to jump up and down right before your eyes. Are you going to argue with that? Are you going to quibble about doctrine?

It's way past time to be dissecting the Word—weighing this phrase against that phrase. Forget all that left-brained nonsense. Just accept the signs. They're billboards pointing the way. You won't go wrong.

People say we don't walk the walk. People say we live an extravagant lifestyle. People even accuse us of fraud. I've got just one answer: Feel the excitement in this room. Feel it. Something is happening here! It's carrying people away. Let it carry you all the way home!

Complacency sets us up. We will fall for the wrong signs if we're stumbling down the easiest path, listening only to the voices that echo our own. The apostle Paul refers to the "lawless one" of the end times as someone who will work "signs and lying wonders." And he says this will result in "all unrighteous deception among those who perish" (2 Thessalonians 2:10). Then he explains *why* these unfortunate people are deceived. They're deceived "because they did not receive the love of the truth, that they might be saved" (verse 10).

These people failed to experience a love of the truth. What does that mean? People who love the truth, respect it as something separate from themselves. Truth is not just what they *want* to believe. Truth is not just a matter of what suits them.

No, to love the truth is to conform to the truth. It's to fit your desires into it, your opinions into it, your attitudes into it. To love the truth is to be molded by the Word of God. You don't shape the truth; it shapes you.

Paul goes on to talk about why people receive a strong delusion, why they believe a lie. He says the bottom line is this: They "did not believe the truth but had pleasure in unrighteousness" (verse 12).

People often lose their love of the truth because they start loving something else. They're clinging to something that's wrong, something unrighteous. So their hold on the truth loosens. They're not comfortable with it. They start putting distance between themselves and conviction. And that's when the false prophet finds easy prey. He offers them all the dazzle without any of the discomfort. He offers to take them to a place they've never been, without their having to grow.

Keep in mind that the false prophet is a special kind of magician. It's not just entertainment he's selling. It's a kind of religion. It's the promise of supernatural solutions to our problems. So we need to be very aware of the kind of faith we give our allegiance to. Not everyone who claims God's endorsement is working on His behalf. Not everyone who speaks the name of Jesus is moved by His Spirit.

We need to ask some hard questions of ourselves, and of any religious group: "Is this group helping me love the truth? Is this group helping me study the Word of God personally? Am I discovering things about myself that need to change? Am I being convicted, as well as comforted?"

I'm afraid many churches today are sliding away from what Jesus and the apostles emphasized. Many churches are making light of God's commandments. Many churches are sidestepping God's eternal law. They may give what appears to be a message of great comfort. But in those nice words, there's the whisper of a false prophet. There's the seductive whisper of someone who tells us only what we want to hear.

A love of the truth is vitally important in the end times. Remember the example of Micaiah. He was willing to listen to *whatever* God said—good news, bad news, or in between. He was willing to go wherever God's truth might lead him.

In the year 250 A.D., when Decius was emperor of Rome, a Christian elder named Pionius was led toward the temple of Nemesis in Smyrna. The city streets were packed with a jeering, holiday crowd. At the temple, an official told the Christian, "You know about the emperor's edict and how it bids you sacrifice to the gods."

Pionius answered calmly, "I know the edicts of God in which He bids us worship Him alone."

Various other officials tried to persuade Pionius to compromise and make sacrifice. He responded, "I wish I could persuade you to be Christians."

They roared with laughter: "You can't make us willing to be burned alive!"

Pionius replied, "It's far worse to be burned when you are dead."

Some bystanders were impressed by Pionius's eloquence as he faced death. They exclaimed, "Ah, what education."

Pionius wanted them to be impressed by something else, "Not that sort of education," he told them. "Recognize, rather, the education of those famines, deaths, and other blows by which you have been tried."

Pionius was referring to some recent disasters in the area. He hoped these people might be moved to look beyond their sorrows to the living God.

His listeners didn't quite get the point, "But you, too, went hungry with us," someone said.

Pionius replied, "But I had hope in God." And he maintained that hope all the way to the end, when he was executed by crucifixion.

The testimony of this little-known believer is just one of many that has come down through the ages to inspire us to love the truth, to love God's truth above all else.

I want to stand with Pionius in the end. I don't want to be swept away by the whisper of the false prophet, just because it's what I want to hear. I want to stand firmly and securely on the foundation of God's truth.

Will you determine to stand with me? Let's stand for truth together. We can begin now, by deciding to listen to whatever God tells us, by committing ourselves to God's whole truth. Just determine to be a good listener. Decide you won't turn away from anything God's Word reveals to you. Decide you'll welcome His commands. Decide you'll take His principles seriously. Decide you'll trust in His promises. Decide you'll meditate on His insights.

That's the key. By clinging to what God has to say you'll find yourself on solid, immovable rock. It won't matter if false prophets are whispering seductively. It won't matter if they can dazzle with wondrous signs.

It won't matter if the crowd is rushing in the wrong direction. You'll know the truth. And you'll know you are free. You'll be able to stand against the tide. Let's pray.

* * * * *

Dear Father, please cure us of complacency. Please help us to be able to hear the hard truths. There are so many competing voices in our world, so many distortions of the truth. Help us to listen carefully to Your Word. Help us to be honest and transparent before it. We thank You for the wonderful good news it reveals. We stake our lives now—and in the future—on the gospel of Jesus Christ. In His name, Amen.

The Rumble of Coercion

We've been looking at Revelation's "Three Most Wanted"—powerful, charismatic figures who play key roles in the drama of the end times. They are its star villains. If God were to put up "wanted" posters on the walls of the universe, these are the three characters you'd see. They represent the most dangerous sins of earth's final days.

Each of the figures in this unholy trinity—the beast, the false prophet, and the dragon—are represented as having unclean spirits, like hideous frogs, coming out of their mouths. All three are eventually thrown into the lake of fire.

In this final chapter, we're going to focus on the third figure in this unholy trinity—the dragon. He's the most dangerous and destructive of all. He's the power behind the scenes and the driving force behind the tragic conflicts that engulf us all.

In this chapter, too, we'll discover how we can keep ourselves and our families safe from his assaults, how we can be sure we're standing in the right place when millions are swept off their feet and into disaster. As we zero in on this third figure—the dragon—we're going to discover just what unclean spirit he manifests, and how we can avoid being seduced and captured by it.

Dragons usually come our way in fairy tales. They pop up in colorful legends. They bellow fiercely. They breathe fire. They threaten some damsel in distress in a castle tower. But there's always a knight in shining armor that arrives in the nick of time. He dodges the fire and manages to thrust his gleaming sword through the dragon's heart.

The final book of the Bible—the book of Revelation—uses this image of a dragon quite differently. It describes something that's anything but something from a fairy tale. The apostle John, writing on the island of Patmos, saw key events at the very end of time. They are certainly larger than life, but they're part of history. They are the climax of history. John uses symbols, but these symbols point to very real forces at work in our world.

Let's start with a bit of background. John shows us how the dragon came to this planet:

> And war broke out in heaven: Michael and his angels fought with the dragon; and the dragon and his angels fought, but they did not prevail, nor was a place found for them in heaven any longer. So the great dragon was cast out, that serpent of old, called the Devil and Satan, who deceives the whole world; he was cast to the earth, and his angels were cast out with him (Revelation 12:7-9).

There you have it. The dragon is none other than Satan himself. Once, in the Garden of Eden, he whispered promises to Eve as a serpent. In the end, he's become a great dragon deceiving the whole world. The dragon is the devil. But let's remember one thing. Satan is the one who is really behind *all* the villains in Revelation. He's driving the beast and the false prophet to act their parts. He's moving through several different figures.

So, this fiery, red dragon represents not just the devil in general; it represents something specific about our ultimate enemy. This symbol is trying to get us to look at a particular way he deceives. Revelation is helping us see exactly what we must avoid at all costs. That's what we're going to uncover. We're going to expose the dangerous sin, the sin that flows out of the dragon's mouth.

Let's take a closer look. What does the dragon actually do? "Now when the dragon saw that he had been cast to the earth, he persecuted the woman who gave birth to the male Child" (verse 13).

The dragon persecutes. Whom does he persecute? A woman. This is the pure woman who represents God's people, the church. The male child, Jesus Christ, came into the world through God's chosen people. The dragon wants to destroy the woman and her child. Why?

Because he's trying to get back at God. Remember Satan made war in heaven. He rebelled, and he lost. He couldn't hurt God. But the war was still going on in his heart. So he tried to hurt God's chosen people. He tried to hurt God's Son. He did it right from the beginning of Jesus' earthly life when Mary gave birth. He worked through tyrannical King Herod who feared the birth of a rival. Herod ordered that every male child in Bethlehem, two years old and under, should be killed.

Mary, Joseph, and the Baby escaped to Egypt. But the dragon kept trying to attack. He kept persecuting. John says, "And the dragon was enraged with the woman, and he went to make war with the rest of her offspring, who keep the commandments of God and have the testimony of Jesus Christ" (verse 17).

The dragon is enraged. He's been hurt. He's been rejected. And he's determined to attack those whom God has accepted, His chosen people. So the devil keeps on making war against the woman's offspring—God's people—until the very end. He will focus his final fury on those who "keep the commandments of God and have the testimony of Jesus Christ" (verse 17).

Now we can see into the dragon's heart. Now we can see just what keeps him breathing fire. It's enmity, pure and simple. It's animosity. It's hatred. The fiery, red dragon represents the compulsion to even the score.

He just can't get over the fact that he was thrown out of heaven. He can't accept that loss. So he expresses the pain and misery inside him by attacking God's children. Revelation describes him as "the accuser of our brethren, who accused them before our God day and night" (verse 10).

The dragon is an accuser. He's been put down; he wants to put everyone else down. He accuses day and night. He's driven on and on by the animosity, the resentment, the jealousy, the rage in his heart.

The dragon represents one of the end time's most dangerous sins. But it's not something that is far, far in the distance. It's not something inhuman. This is an "unclean spirit" that can get quite comfortable in the human heart. Once animosity gets in the door, it can start rearranging our whole lives. It takes over. A little spot of resentment can grow and grow until it eats up our hearts.

And do you know when malice is most dangerous? When you're sure you've been wronged; when you're positive you're in the right—that's when it takes root. You think you're crusading for justice. You think you're just trying to make things fair. You think you have the truth on your side. But guess what? Inside your passionate speeches, there's the sound of a dragon; there's the rumble of coercion; there's a fire that will consume you.

When people see someone, or some group, as "the enemy," they tend to focus their lives on that enemy. Everything gets drawn into the conflict. Everything is win/lose. Everything is about getting the upper hand.

The apostle John, who wrote Revelation, also wrote three short letters in the New Testament. And in those letters we find him writing about the consequences of malice. He shows us the end of the road for those who focus on an enemy. What he's really warning us about is the sin of the dragon.

He says, "He who says he is in the light, and hates his brother, is in darkness . . . (he) walks in darkness, and does not know where he is going, because the darkness has blinded his eyes" (1 John 2:9, 11).

Jesus once warned about those who are thrown out of God's great banquet at the end of the age. They occupy an outer darkness where there is weeping and gnashing of teeth. Well, John is telling us what that darkness is made of. It's made of hatred. It's made of animosity and resentment cherished in the heart. It's made of enemies.

We can make all the claims to being right that we want. We can say that we have the light and the truth. But if we cherish hatred, we're stumbling in the dark. We're out of touch. We're clueless about grace.

Why is animosity one of the most dangerous sins in the end time? John tells us exactly why: "He who does not love does not know God, for God is love." (1 John 4:8).

That's clear enough, isn't it? You want to be in God's circle of love now. You want to be there in the last days. You don't want to be caught up in a campaign to accuse; you don't want to be consumed by your plots against an enemy.

It's important to keep one thing in mind, however, about this particular last day peril. The dragon's hatred isn't something that's thrown in our faces. It doesn't come to us as an ugly roar. Remember that Satan disguises himself as an angel of light. The dragon figure is part of a false religious system called Babylon. He leads a movement that sweeps millions in its wake. He compels allegiance.

So, we have to ask ourselves: How does hatred become seductive? How does animosity become attractive, clothed in religious garments?

It happened in a very big way during the Crusades of the Middle Ages. Christians were persuaded that defending the faith meant attacking the Saracens who possessed Jerusalem. It seemed like a great cause, a great calling. And it ended up in the worst kind of slaughter of Muslims in the Holy Land.

Even today, religion is being used to motivate people to commit acts of terror. They think they are part of a great cause. They think they are defending the faith against its enemies. They are seduced by the rumble of coercion. And they end up slaughtering innocent individuals in the name of God.

This rumble is the rumble of a dragon. It's a sound Revelation warns us about. Take a look at Revelation 13. Here we see the antichrist powers begin to enforce their faith. They cause "as many as would not worship the image of the beast to be killed" (verse 15). Coercion. It's the dragon's way. It's Satan's way. It's what malice in the heart leads us to.

Let's take a look at another symbol in the book of Revelation. In chapter 17 we encounter a harlot named Babylon. She represents false religious systems. This is what the apostle John writes: "I saw the woman, drunk with the blood of the saints and with the blood of the martyrs of Jesus" (verse 6).

Yes, that's the end of the line for malice. Hatred must have enemies; it must have victims. False religious systems use force. False religious systems use pressure. False religious systems use coercion. And eventually they will end up slaughtering the followers of Christ— in the name of God!

In describing this unholy trinity—the evil powers of the end time—John writes: " 'These will make war with the Lamb' " (verse 14). They may claim to speak for the

Lamb of God, but they make war against Him. They may say nice things about the Lamb of God, but they make war against Him. They may tell you over and over that the truth is on their side, but they make war against the Lamb.

Friends, in the last days, the dragon will use religion to harness hatred in a powerful way. Only it won't seem like hatred at all. It will seem like people are defending the faith. It will seem like people are battling for the truth. The dragon will use religion to persecute those who "keep the commandments of God and have the testimony of Jesus Christ" (Revelation 12:17). The dragon will make up his own commands to set aside the clear teaching of Scripture. The dragon will use human traditions to deny the prophetic voice of God. And finally, the dragon will focus his followers on a scapegoat—a group that is accused of being to blame for all the world's problems. "They're different," the dragon will say. "They don't conform. They cling to beliefs that we know have been superseded. They're not willing to give in to the majority."

Religion can indeed be used that way. It can be used to demonize. It can back up the murmur of malice. It can exploit what's been festering in our hearts.

We need an alternative to the animosity that can eat us alive. We need protection from the rumble of coercion. We need to make sure we don't get swept up in a religious movement that will end up persecuting the remnant of God's people, the faithful in the end times.

Again, the apostle John shows us the safe ground on which to stand. "He who loves his brother abides in the light, and there is no cause for stumbling in him" (1 John 2:10). There it is. Do you want to make sure you abide in the light? Love your brother. Make sure love is at the center of your faith. Make sure love is at the center of your God. Make sure love is at the center of all you do in His name. Love is the only answer to coercion—love for Christ, love for one another, love for the truth. That's the answer.

Without love, Paul tells us, we become just noisy gongs and clanging cymbals (see 1 Corinthians 13:1). Without love we aren't building anything worthwhile. Without love we will fall for the rumble of coercion; we'll become trapped by the dragon's unclean spirit.

In his Gospel, John records Jesus' words on love as the place of safety. "If you keep My commandments, you will abide in My love, just as I have kept My Father's commandments and abide in His love" (John 15:10). Love moves us to obey. It moves us to conform our lives to God's commandments. The dragon tries to draw people away from God's commandments in order to draw them away from God's love. He wants people stuck in malice.

Back during World War II, a young woman named Margaret Covell had every reason to be overwhelmed by malice. Her missionary parents were killed by Japanese soldiers in the Philippines. At first, Margaret was choked by hatred for the Japanese. But slowly she pieced together details about her mom's and dad's last moments. As they had knelt before the drawn swords of their captors, their lips had been moving. Their last words were a prayer for their executioners.

Margaret kept thinking about the love that had moved her parents to serve God, and she made a decision. She walked up to a Japanese prisoner of war camp in America and volunteered her services as a social worker. For months she ministered to the needs of former Japanese soldiers with kindness and tireless energy. These men had been trained to treat their enemies with contempt. So they were perplexed by her conscientious care. They asked her why she took such pains with them.

So she told them about her parents. Now they were really dumfounded. One man who later heard her story was Mitsuo Fuchida. He'd led the attack on Pearl Harbor, but had become bitter and disillusioned at war's end. In fact, he was determined to prove that the Americans were just as cruel with their prisoners of war as the Japanese had been.

But Margaret Covell's example left him deeply shaken. It forced him to think about life from an entirely new perspective. And in the end he made a commitment to this love that shines out of the gospel of Jesus Christ. Mr. Fuchida became a well-known evangelist in his country that persuaded many of his fellow citizens to exchange hurt and hatred for the sacrificial love of God.

Margaret shows us where to stand when all the voices around us are filled with rage and resentment. She shows us what taking the love of Christ seriously can do—even in the worst of times.

I want to stand with people like Margaret Covell. I want to stand with believers down through the ages who have resisted the rumble of coercion and who have proclaimed an allegiance to unconditional love. I want to express my love for God by following His commandments, by staying close to Jesus, by accepting His forgiveness and grace.

And I want you to stand in that same circle of love—now and in the final days of history. Let's make that commitment together. Don't let any movement, however popular, don't let any voice, however loud, draw you away from a simple and pure devotion to Christ. His love is all we need. His love will keep us safe. His love will lead us home.

* * * * *

Dear Father, we want to place Your love at the center of our lives. Please keep us from animosity and resentment. Please root these things out of our hearts. We don't want to give the devil that foothold. We don't want to listen to the murmur of animosity. We want to hear Your gracious voice. We want to build on Your forgiveness. We want to be guided by Your commandments. Thank You for laying down Your life on the cross to make our place of safety possible. Thank You for accepting us as Your children. And so keep us sitting at Your feet. In the name of Jesus we ask it. Amen.

FREE Bible Reading Guides

Call toll free
1-800-253-3000
or mail the coupon below
Today!

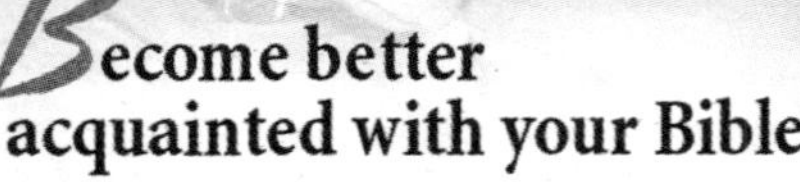

*B*ecome better acquainted with your Bible

- *No cost now or in the future.*
- *Designed especially for busy people like you.*
- *Study at home.*
- *These guides will bring the Bible to life.*

☐ **Yes!** Please send me the 26 **FREE** Bible Reading Guides.

Name ___________________________

Address _________________________

City ____________________________

State/Province _____________ Zip/Postal Code _____________

Please mail this completed coupon to: **DISCOVER**

it is written · Box O · Thousand Oaks, CA 91360